Stars

BEFORE BEDTIME

A MINDFUL FALL-ASLEEP BOOK

WRITTEN BY
CLAIRE GRACE & DR. JESSAMY HIBBERD

ILLUSTRATED BY
HANNAH TOLSON

HOW TO READ THIS BOOK
(FOR GROWN-UPS)

Sleep can be hard to come by in our hyper-stimulating modern world.
Bedtime routines, including reading together, can help. Each page in this book contains
relaxation exercises that are woven into stories about the magical night sky.

Look out for the moon symbol to find the exercises.

Each exercise is short and simple to do. The pages are self-contained, so there is no need to read
through from beginning to end if you don't want to. To start with, try to complete just
two or three exercises—the key is for the child to enjoy it and for it not to feel like a chore.
If they've had enough after one, then stop. If they want to keep going, then read another.

Try every strategy, even the ones you think your child might not like. There's no "one size fits
all," so it's important to figure out what works for you and the child. Different approaches work
for different people, and by trying out all the strategies, you'll find a range of options.

Try and join in with the exercises, as modeling is a great
way to help children learn. You'll have the added bonus of a
relaxing end to your day and you might even
pick up a few that work for you!

The sky is full of sparkling little lights blinking back at us. There are trillions of stars up above, and they all have their own wonderful story to tell.

A group of stars is called a CONSTELLATION. This just means that they form a pattern that tells a story. The patterns they make sometimes look like animals, mythical creatures, people, and gods.

People have been telling stories about these sparkling constellations for years on end. Get comfortable, and say goodbye to the wriggles and the fidgets. It's time to settle down, quiet your mind, and let the calm feelings in.

LET'S JOURNEY THROUGH THE DEEP, DARK NIGHT SKY.

Do you recognize the constellation of ORION THE HUNTER? He stands proudly in the night sky holding his enormous shield and sword. Near to Orion are two dogs, CANIS MAJOR and CANIS MINOR, who are whizzing through the glittering sky together as they try to catch LEPUS THE HARE.

Can you make your body look like a hare? Place your hands and knees on your mattress so that you're on all fours. Move your feet together so that your two big toes touch. Lower your butt toward your heels and stretch your arms out in front of you—as if they were long hare ears. Gently place your forehead on the mattress and let your chest sink down between your knees. Take three deep, slow breaths in and out.

Lepus jumps and soars as she tries to outrun Orion the Hunter and his dogs. Her big feet go thump, thump, thump.

Now lie back, place your hand on your heart, and feel it beating. Thump, thump, thump. Take a deep breath in and blow out.

HYDRA
the Serpent

AQUILA
the Eagle

The ancient Greeks saw birds in the night sky, such as big, strong AQUILA THE EAGLE and naughty CORVUS THE CROW. They would tell the story of the god Apollo, who asked the crow to fetch him some water as quickly as possible. On his way to get water, the crow spotted a fig tree and sat for hours greedily filling his belly with fruit. Realizing he was going to be in trouble for being late, the crow lied to Apollo and told him that THE SERPENT HYDRA had blocked the spring so he couldn't get any water. But Apollo didn't believe his lies, and flung the crow up into the sky to be trapped there forever.

Stretch your arms out as wide as you can, like wings, and take a deep breath in. As you breathe out, picture yourself soaring across the night sky like an eagle. With your eyes still closed, place your hands on your belly and take a deep breath in. Fill your belly with air so it gets big and fat like Corvus's did when he filled it with fruit. Can you feel your breath there? Now breathe out, let it go, and feel the air leaving your tummy. Do this three times.

DRACO the Dragon

There are lots of tales told about this twisting, slithering, snake-like constellation. One story says that DRACO is a dragon that guarded a tree heavy with golden apples. The great hero HERCULES fought Draco to steal the apples as part of 12 tasks he had to perform—these were called his 12 Labors. With no stars making wings or legs, Draco's shape looks more like a snake than a dragon! What do you think?

Stretch out in your bed to make
yourself as long as a snake.
Take a deep breath in through your
nose and then breathe out all the air
through your mouth while you make a
hissing noise, just like a slithering snake.
Hisssssss!

HISSSSSS!

Have you ever seen a "W" constellation in the night sky? It is called CASSIOPEIA. She was a queen from the Greek myths, who thought she was the most beautiful woman in the world—even more beautiful than the gods! The gods were not happy about her saying this and sent a monster to attack Cassiopeia's kingdom. As punishment for Cassiopeia's vanity, she was placed among the stars, where she sits today, combing her long hair. Her husband, CEPHEUS THE KING, sits in the sky near his wife, along with their daughter, ANDROMEDA THE PRINCESS, who wears a glittering crown.

Can you picture a golden crown in your mind? Hold out your hand in front of you and pretend it is a crown. Trace up the side of your thumb and breathe in while you do this. Now trace down the other side of your thumb and breathe out. Do this to the rest of your fingers, remembering to breathe in and out as you move up and down each finger.

Another Greek tale told of how the god Zeus changed into a swan to get the attention of Queen Leda of Sparta. Zeus pretended he was being attacked by an eagle and dove into Leda's arms for protection. The couple had two children together, and to celebrate their births, Zeus placed a swan among the stars. That swan is the constellation CYGNUS.

Near Cygnus is a cluster of faint stars that look like a **LITTLE FOX** leaping through the sky with his bushy tail reaching out behind him as he runs through a deep green forest.

VULPECULA
the Little Fox

CYGNUS
the Swan

Can you imagine a special place in your mind that gives you a feeling of safety and calm? Perhaps you are floating on a calm pond, like a swan. Or maybe you are walking through a beautiful green forest like a little fox? Can you see little rays of sunlight dancing on the ground around you? Can you feel the wind on your face and smell the fresh air? Can you hear the rustle of the leaves on the trees? Is anyone you love there with you? Imagine exploring your safe space. Would you climb the trees, look for bugs, or make an amazing den? Use your imagination to make it exactly right for you.

On a very dark night, you might be able to see a shimmering, cloudy band of stars crossing the night sky. This is called the Milky Way, and it is a collection of stars, dust, and gases in space. At the center of the Milky Way is the constellation SAGITTARIUS, THE ARCHER. With the body of a horse and the torso of a man, Sagittarius was a centaur and is usually shown as being very strong with powerful muscles, pulling his bow back to fire an arrow. Can you imagine being as strong and fast as a horse?

SAGITTARIUS
the Archer

You have muscles all over your body. Let's try tensing and then relaxing them. Take a deep breath in and clench your fists as tight as you can. Now let out all the air and release your fists. Tense up your arms and release, remembering to take a big breath in and out as you squeeze and release. Pull your shoulders up to your ears and release. Wrinkle up your nose, scrunch up your eyes and your face, and then release. Clench your jaw and then unclench it. Tighten your stomach so it feels all hard and then let go. Now squeeze your bottom and then let it go. Finally, scrunch up your legs and toes and then stretch them apart. Feel how your whole body is relaxed now. Notice how nice it feels.

Part of this constellation is shaped like a saucepan. It's called THE GREAT BEAR, which is odd because this constellation has a long tail—and bears don't have long tails! One story says that Zeus fell in love again, this time with a beautiful nymph named Callisto. But Zeus's wife found out about their love and turned Callisto into a bear. To protect Callisto, Zeus sent her into the sky, where she sparkles through the night.

Near the Great Bear is another constellation, THE LITTLE BEAR. This is home to a very important star called POLARIS or "the North Star." This incredibly bright star was used by sailors to find their way home if they ever got lost at sea.

Close your eyes and picture the bright star of Polaris in your head. Imagine it traveling slowly down all of your body— from your head right down to your tippy-toes.

Let's take a trip to the zoo in the sky. Look out for CAMELOPARDALIS THE GIRAFFE with his long neck, APUS THE BIRD OF PARADISE with her colorful, feathery tail billowing out behind her, LACERTA THE LIZARD as he scampers across the sky, and big-eyed CHAMAELEON THE CHAMELEON with his long, sticky, tongue. Chamaeleon the Chameleon isn't very bright and can be difficult to find. This might be why it's named after the camouflaging chameleon, which can change color to blend in with its surroundings.

CAMELOPARDALIS
the Giraffe

CHAMAELEON
the Chameleon

APUS
the Bird of
Paradise

LACERTA
the Lizard

Imagine a color that makes you feel warm, happy, and safe. What color are you thinking of? Close your eyes and picture that color surrounding you. Imagine it entering through your heart and flowing slowly through your body, filling you with warmth, strength, and happiness.

Have you ever seen the constellation GEMINI glittering in the sky? This group of stars looks like two people holding hands. The brightest stars in the constellation are named after twin characters from Greek mythology named Castor and Pollux.

Hold your hands together just like Castor and Pollux. Rest them on your chest—can you feel your breath moving in and out as your chest rises and falls?

GEMINI
the Twins

The twins helped save their sister Helen after she was kidnapped. They mounted their horses and charged into the Greek city of Attica to rescue her and bring her home.

Think of someone you love. Close your eyes and picture them as clearly as you can. Bring a smile to your face and imagine them watching over you.

In ancient Greek stories, ARIES THE RAM was covered in glittering golden wool. A hero named Jason went on a long and dangerous journey to try and capture the golden fleece. He traveled here, there, and everywhere on his trusty ship, ARGO NAVIS, to try and get the shimmering fleece.

ARIES
the Ram

Close your eyes and picture the ship in your head. Now climb on board and let's go on an adventure. You are the captain of the ship. Feel as the boat swoops and turns as you whiz past the stars. Are you going fast or are you traveling slowly? What do you see as you sail across the sky? Now take a deep breath and breathe out slowly as you glide your ship back down to the ground when you're ready. Stop very gently. Breathe in deeply and then exhale.

ARGO NAVIS
the Ship

Have you ever heard about a mythical firebird called a PHOENIX? Stories say that every couple of hundred years the bird builds a little nest for itself where it then bursts into beautiful orange, red, and yellow colored flames. Then, from the ashes, a little baby phoenix is reborn and lives again for another couple of hundred years before the whole process starts again.

PHOENIX
the Firebird

Can you imagine a beautiful red phoenix feather? Close your eyes and picture it as clearly as you can. Now hold up one finger in front of your mouth and pretend it is the feather. Take a deep breath in through your nose. As you breathe out, blow the air out through your mouth very slowly and softly. Feel the air on your finger and imagine the feather fluttering as you blow on it. Breathe in slowly through your nose and repeat three times.

Good night, Stars

The night sky is full of mystery, adventure, and age-old tales. We've journeyed all around the dark and glittering night sky, but now it's time to snuggle deep beneath our covers, close our eyes, and let these magical stories fill our dreams.

Maybe you'll dream of floating through a moonlit sky on broad wings, like Aquila the Eagle. Or perhaps you'll drift down a glittering stream with Cygnus the Swan.

Close your eyes, burrow beneath your blankets, and let your dreams whisk you away on a magical starry adventure.

NOTES FOR GROWN-UPS

The mind and body are pretty amazing. They are constantly sending messages to each other and working together to look after you and keep you healthy. They are intimately linked, and the simplest route to calming your mind is to start by checking in with your body and trying to relax it.

Regularly practicing breathing exercises, muscle tension and release, relaxation and stretches, as well as imagery and mindfulness, can help improve sleep, decrease stress and anxiety, strengthen immunity, and increase happiness, optimism, and well-being long-term.

The exercises in this book will help prepare children for a good night's sleep but will also help them in lots of other areas of life. The world is full of stressed-out adults (who frequently ignore what their bodies are trying to tell them), so teaching children at a young age how to breathe, ground themselves, tune in to the present, and slow down their thoughts will help prepare them for the future and set them up with tools and techniques for how to live in an often fast-paced world.

Brimming with creative inspiration, how-to projects, and useful information to enrich your everyday life, Quarto Knows is a favorite destination for those pursuing their interests and passions. Visit our site and dig deeper with our books into your area of interest: Quarto Creates, Quarto Cooks, Quarto Homes, Quarto Lives, Quarto Drives, Quarto Explores, Quarto Gifts, or Quarto Kids.

Inspiring | Educating | Creating | Entertaining

First published in 2020 by Wide Eyed Editions, an imprint of The Quarto Group.
The Old Brewery, 6 Blundell Street, London N7 9BH, United Kingdom.
T (0)20 7700 6700 F (0)20 7700 8066 www.QuartoKnows.com

A catalog record for this book is available from the British Library.

ISBN 978-0-7112-5557-9

The illustrations were created digitally
Set in Futura, Amatic SC and Print Bold

Published by Georgia Amson-Bradshaw and Katie Cotton
Designed by Myrto Dimitrakoulia
Edited by Claire Grace
Production by Dawn Cameron

Manufactured in: Guangdong, China CC122019

9 8 7 6 5 4 3 2 1